First Facts™

American Symbols

The U.S. Capitol

by Terri DeGezelle

Consultant:
Melodie Andrews, Ph.D.
Associate Professor of Early American History
Minnesota State University, Mankato

Capstone
press

Mankato, Minnesota

First Facts is published by Capstone Press,
151 Good Counsel Drive, P.O. Box 669, Mankato, Minnesota 56002.
www.capstonepress.com

Library of Congress Cataloging-in-Publication Data
DeGezelle, Terri, 1955–
    The U.S. Capitol / by Terri DeGezelle.
    p. cm.—(American symbols)
    Includes bibliographical references (p. 24) and index.
    Contents: U.S. Capitol fast facts—American symbol of democracy—The contest—Building the Capitol—War and rebuilding—Changes to the Capitol—The Capitol and the Civil War—The U.S. Capitol today—Timeline—Hands on: make a Capitol model
    ISBN-13: 978-0-7368-2294-7 (hardcover)   ISBN-10: 0-7368-2294-1 (hardcover)
    ISBN-13: 978-0-7368-4990-6 (softcover pbk.)   ISBN-10: 0-7368-4990-4 (softcover pbk.)
    1. United States Capitol (Washington, D.C.)—Juvenile literature. 2. Washington (D.C.)—Buildings, structures, etc.—Juvenile literature. [1. United States Capitol (Washington, D.C.) 2. Washington (D.C.)—Buildings, structures, etc.] I. Title. II. Series.
F204 .C2.D4 2004
975.3—dc21
    2002156497

Editorial Credits

Roberta Schmidt, editor; Linda Clavel, designer; Kelly Garvin, photo researcher;
    Eric Kudalis and Karen Risch, product planning editors

Photo Credits

Bruce Coleman Inc./Werner Bertsch, cover
Corbis, 17; Corbis/Bettmann, 12
Digital Vision, 5
Index Stock Imagery/Mark Reinstein, 7
Library of Congress, 9, 11, 15, 20
North Wind Picture Archives, 13
Stock Montage, Inc., 16
U.S. Postal Service, 19 (top), 21
U.S. Treasury, 19 (bottom)

2 3 4 5 6 08 07 06 05 04

Table of Contents

U.S. Capitol Fast Facts

- The United States Capitol building in Washington, D.C., is a symbol of democracy.

- Dr. William Thornton won a contest for his design of the Capitol building. He was a medical doctor from the British West Indies.

- The Capitol covers an area slightly larger than four football fields. It is 751 feet (229 meters) long, 350 feet (107 meters) wide, and has 540 rooms.

- The U.S. Congress meets in the Capitol. Congress is made up of the Senate and the House of Representatives.

- Statues and artwork in the Capitol show important events in U.S. history.

American Symbol of Democracy

The United States Capitol building is a symbol of democracy. In a democracy, people choose their leaders by voting. The U.S. Congress meets in the Capitol building. Members of Congress make new laws for the United States.

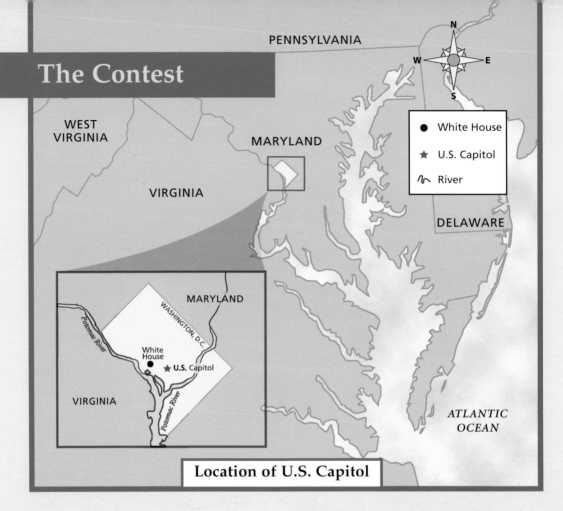

Location of U.S. Capitol

The U.S. Capitol is in Washington, D.C. In 1790, Congress held a contest to find a design for the Capitol building. Dr. William Thornton won the contest. His design looked like a Roman temple. It reminded people that Romans set up one of the first democracies. The new Capitol building would stand for American democracy.

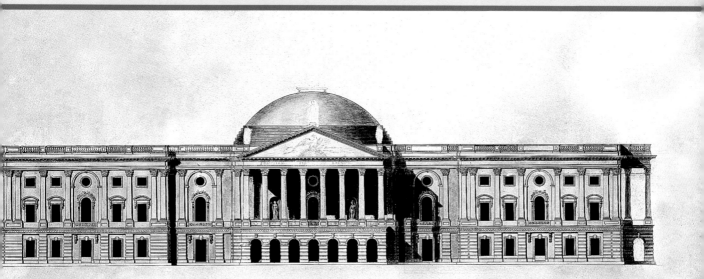

Building the Capitol

In 1793, President George Washington laid the cornerstone for the Capitol. The north wing of the building was finished in 1800. The Senate meets there. The south wing was completed in 1811. This wing is home to the House of Representatives.

cornerstone

the first brick or stone of a building that is going to be built

War and Rebuilding

During the War of 1812 (1812–1814), British soldiers set fire to the Capitol. Everything inside the building burned.

Fire and smoke turned the building's walls black. Workers started to rebuild the Capitol in 1815. By 1819, the Capitol was ready for Congress to meet there again.

Changes to the Capitol

Changes were made to the Capitol in the 1800s. In 1818, work began on the central part of the Capitol. Workers built a large circle-shaped hall. They covered the hall with a dome. In the 1850s, new buildings were added onto the north and south wings.

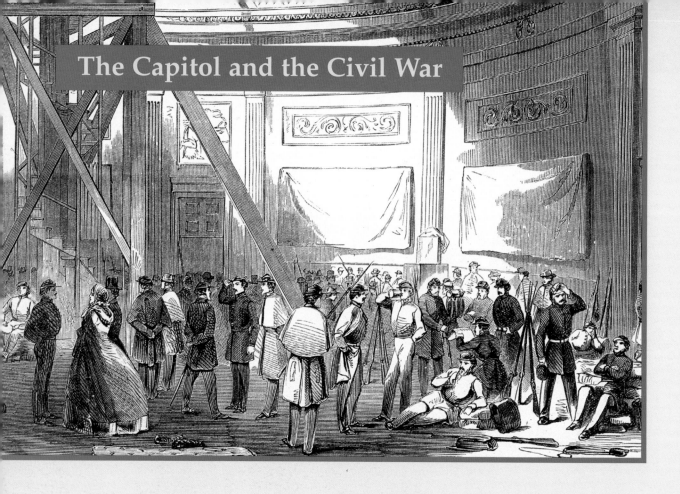

Soldiers lived in the Capitol during the Civil War (1861–1865). Part of the building was used as a hospital. The basement was used to bake bread for the troops.

Work on the Capitol continued during the war. A larger dome was built. In 1863, a statue called *Freedom* was placed on top of the dome.

The U.S. Capitol Today

The Capitol is still the home of Congress. Part of the Capitol is also a museum. The building is shown on postage stamps. It is also on the back of the $50 bill. The U.S. Capitol continues to stand for democracy.

museum

a place where visitors can see historical objects and art

Timeline

1793—Dr. William Thornton wins the contest for his design of the U.S. Capitol.

1814—British troops set fire to the Capitol.

1790—Congress holds a contest for the Capitol building's design.

1793—George Washington lays the cornerstone of the building.

1863—The statue *Freedom* is placed on top of the Capitol dome.

1815—Workers start to rebuild the Capitol.

1901—The first postage stamp to picture the Capitol is printed.

Hands On: Make a Capitol Model

Buildings can have many shapes. You can see some of the different shapes in the U.S. Capitol's building by doing this activity.

What You Need

Large rectangle of white paper
Piece of construction paper
Glue
Square of white paper
Half circle of white paper
Small rectangle of white paper

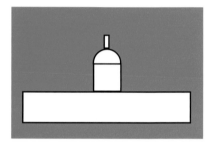

What You Do

1. Put the large rectangle on the bottom of the construction paper. Glue it into place. This rectangle is the bottom of your U.S. Capitol model.
2. Glue the square above the middle of the rectangle. This square is part of the Capitol dome.
3. Put the half circle above the square. Glue it into place. This half circle is the top of the Capitol dome.
4. Glue the small rectangle above the half circle. This rectangle is the statue *Freedom*.

Words to Know

Congress (KONG-griss)—the branch of the U.S. government that makes laws

democracy (di-MOK-ruh-see)—a government in which people choose their leaders by voting

design (di-ZINE)—a plan of something that could be built

dome (DOHM)—a roof shaped like half of a ball

statue (STACH-oo)—something carved or shaped out of stone, wood, or other material

symbol (SIM-buhl)—an object that stands for something else

temple (TEM-puhl)—a building used for worship

Read More

Britton, Tamara L. *The Capitol.* Symbols, Landmarks, and Monuments. Edina, Minn.: Abdo, 2003.

Reef, Catherine. *The United States Capitol.* Places in American History. New York: Dillon Press, 2000.

Internet Sites

Do you want to find out more about the U.S. Capitol? Let FactHound, our fact-finding hound dog, do the research for you.

Here's how:
1. Visit *http://www.facthound.com*
2. Type in the **Book ID** number:
   0736822941
3. Click on **FETCH IT**.

FactHound will fetch Internet sites picked by our editors just for you!

Index